From the Author's Desk . . .

Dear Reader:

As a teenager in the 1970s, my personal hero was Steve Martin. I admired his singular brand of comedy – his twisted intellectual insights, his goofball physical slapstick, his banjo playing, and the whole schtick that he invented as a comedian who was funny simply because he *thought* he was funny.

In 1979, I went to see Steve Martin at the Kemper Arena in Kansas City, Mo. This was during the "wild and crazy guy" fervor that he and Dan Aykroyd had created on Saturday Night Live.

There was an opening act, which I cannot remember. But I do remember the crowd – thousands of people, like a rock concert – getting restless. They started to chant, "We want Steve!".

The stage went dark for a minute. Suddenly, "King Tut," Steve Martin's hit song, blared out over the loud speakers. The crowd went wild as he came on stage in his white suit. And he kept us all entertained for almost two hours.

But what amazed me the most – what has stuck with me all these years – was the *transition* that he sparked from a dark, quiet stage to a wildly excited audience.

I was so inspired that I even tried my own hand at stand-up comedy, entering several talent shows as a teenager. That's when I developed a keen appreciation for Groucho Marx's purported deathbed quote: "Dying is easy. *Comedy* is hard."

What does this have to do with turning around troubled IT projects? Well, at the core of my soul, there is a desire to make people laugh – especially after they've endured the frustration and anxiety which often accompany troubled projects.

I am not always successful at getting the laughs (Groucho was right). And I'm sure that many of the laughs that I *have* gotten were related to my being the guy in charge, or simply being the guy who was funny because he *thought* he was funny.

But, as Steve Martin taught me, that's OK.

For me, the most gratifying moments of turning around troubled projects have occurred during the transition period between doubt and hope. That's when everyone starts to believe that the project has traction and momentum. That's when the team starts laughing again, and they begin to invest themselves more fully into the success of the project.

And, the way I see it, if this turnaround gig ever gets too hard, I can always go back to stand-up. It's like Groucho once said: "The great thing about comedy is that if you fail, no one will laugh at you."

Sincerely,

Shane A. Hills

P.S. This book is designed to be a quick, 40-page "airplane read," providing you with immediately actionable take-away. If you like this book, please share it with a friend. If you don't like it, please share it with someone you don't like.

Mark Twain's Secret for Tackling Big Projects

"The secret of getting ahead is getting started. The secret of getting started is breaking your complex, overwhelming tasks into small, manageable tasks, and then starting on the first one."

- Mark Twain, 1835-1910, who used this approach to write great American novels such as *Tom Sawyer* and *The Adventures of Huckleberry Finn*

Change Is Difficult and Dangerous

"There is nothing so difficult to take in hand, more perilous to conduct, more uncertain in its success, than to take the lead in the introduction of a new order of things."

- Niccolo Machiavelli, Italian statesman, from *The Prince*, 1531

Table of Contents

Industry Facts to Consider about Project Failure

More than two-thirds of IT projects deliver poor results. The most widely used measure of IT project failure is the CHAOS Report from the Standish Group (Boston, MA). The report is based on a worldwide survey of several thousand medium-to-large companies. Results of the 2009 survey indicated that only 32 percent of IT projects were considered "successful"; 24 percent were considered outright failures; and 44 percent were significantly challenged.

More than 70 percent of enterprise "change" initiatives fail. For enterprise-wide change initiatives, which often involve a significant IT component, it is estimated that 70 percent or more fail to be adopted within the organization. According to John Kotter, a Harvard professor and author of the book *Leading Change*, one of the most pervasive causes of this problem is simply the lack of a "sense of urgency."

Large projects may be destined to fail. Jim Johnson, chairman of The Standish Group, was quoted in CIO Magazine in 2007: "Seventy-three percent of projects with labor cost of less than $750,000 succeed. But only 3 percent of projects a with labor cost of over $10 million succeed. I would venture to say the 3 percent that succeed succeeded because they overestimated their budget, not because they were managed properly."

Intervention *works*. According to a study by the Center for Business Practices in Havertown, PA, entitled *Troubled Projects: Project Failure or Project Recovery*, organizations which had a standardized recovery process experienced an 83% higher project success rate than those which did not. The study considered about 4,000 projects over a 12-month period. The study also revealed that project recovery interventions were highly successful and typically involved redefining the project, changing leadership on the project, adding resources and improving project management practices.

"Failure" is not always an accurate word. In a report released by Forrester Research in July 2008, *Debunking IT Project Failure Myths*, the traditional measures of project success (on-time, within budget, and with the initially expected requirements) sets IT departments up for failure. Because IT projects tend to involve unknown complexities, requirements and integration challenges, the initial estimates for schedule, budget and requirements are dangerously volatile. The business sponsors tend to fix their expectations on the original estimates, yet the project plan and the communication about the project tends to significantly lag the reality of new discoveries along the way.

Who Is the Audience for this Book?

This book applies to everyone involved with a Guerrilla project, although some passages will resonate more with executives than project managers. Multiple audiences are addressed because the success of a Guerrilla project depends on the collaboration of several key participants, such as . . .

- An **Executive Champion** who stands behind the project, assists in removing roadblocks, and enlists the cooperation of other groups when needed
- A **Guerrilla Project Manager** who provides genuine leadership, exercises superior soft skills and boldly faces the tougher measures inherent on a recovery project
- A **Project Team** which can suspend its disbelief, give the Guerrilla PM the room he or she needs to drive the project and collaborate to build a solution, and . . .
- **Stakeholders** who are open-minded, focused on the future and willing to re-consider fundamental aspects of the project such as scope, schedule and cost

This book is a primer serving to inform all participants on what to expect from a project recovery (hereafter referred to as a "Guerrilla project"). This book is designed to be an "airplane read" – cutting to the chase quickly – which is a quality essential to the success of a Guerrilla project.

Although important details are included (such as flowcharts for a Basic Turnaround and a SWAT Team Turnaround), this book does not attempt to provide in-depth instructions on how to implement a recovery.

For the purpose of training Guerrilla Project Managers, there are workshops available. Additionally, there are several lengthy books on project recovery listed in the Bibliography.

The term "Guerrilla" is used interchangeably with "turnaround" or "recovery" in this book.

**Use this Book as a Launching Pad to Help Point
Troubled Projects in the Right Direction**

The approach described in this book is offered as a framework only. No two Guerrilla projects will be exactly alike, but this book can be used as a launching pad to help you determine what to do next. Further, no Guerrilla project will ever be perfect. But even the partial implementation of Guerrilla principles can be enough to restore momentum and achieve success on troubled IT projects.

What is Guerrilla Project Management?

In the coal mines of the late 19th and early 20th centuries, canaries were used to alert the miners when dangerous levels of explosive methane gas had polluted the air. Perched in bird cages hanging from overhead beams, the canaries would chirp and flutter when the air was safe. When the air was dangerous, the canaries would stop chirping, sway on their perches and drop dead. Using this as their warning signal, the miners would scramble quickly out of the mine shaft and back to safety.

Unfortunately, in today's world of highly complex IT projects, we have yet to invent a warning system which matches the reliability of a canary in a coal mine. Even in the most advanced organizations, with well-rooted Project Management Offices (PMOs) and strong executive leadership, the harbingers of impending project collapse can occasionally be overlooked or ignored.

Reams of literature have been written about project management processes and software development methodologies. The tools for managing projects have become increasingly more sophisticated and robust. Thousands of organizations have implemented some form of a PMO. And, according to the Project Management Institute (PMI), more than 200,000 people have earned certification as a Project Management Professional (PMP®).

A Guerrilla Project is 90% about People, and 10% about Technology

> Most of the development, database and infrastructure platforms that we use today are mature, reliable and relatively straight-forward. When an IT project drifts toward the rocks, the issues are rarely technical. Instead, it is more likely that communication has faltered, expectations have become misaligned, and stakeholders have become fatigued or disengaged. To redeem these issues requires a strategy for intervention, advanced skills in people care, and a swift restoration of order. Once these issues have been addressed, the technical talent on your team can thrive.

Despite these advances, more than two thirds of IT projects fail to deliver as expected. High-profile project failures in organizations as diverse as Nike, Nestlé, the IRS and the FBI—costing hundreds of millions of dollars—have made headlines in the media.

This book, although written by a PMP®, does not advise you on how to manage a project under normal circumstances. Instead, this book starts where most of the literature stops: What to do when an organization's standard methodology fails to deliver as expected, and a critical project stands in jeopardy.

A seriously troubled project often cannot be fixed using the same methodology and management structure under which it faltered. Browbeating the project team can exacerbate the problems and put the project at greater risk. Further, to replace the project manager is typically an insufficient measure. On most of the projects for which I have been asked to intervene, the project manager has already been replaced — sometimes more than once.

We simply live in a more complex world today than we did 30 years ago. We communicate worldwide and instantaneously. Technology obsoletes itself rapidly. Business dynamics and cultural shifts can change the marketplace, seemingly overnight. Consider, for example, how Wal-Mart — well on its way to becoming the world's first trillion-dollar company — has demanded greater efficiency from its suppliers. Consider the pervasive existence of Amazon, eBay, Google, Facebook and the Internet in general, and how it has changed our expectations of customer service, availability of product and access to information.

Today's projects are fraught with increasing complexity, unpredictable changes and a high-margin for error — all the canaries of our project management coal mine. With projects moving at such high velocity, it's not uncommon to overlook the warning signs before it's too late for simple fixes.

What "Guerrilla" Means in the Context of a Turnaround Project

Although Guerrilla Project Management (GPM) is based on lean principles, it is *not* an excuse to attempt to do too much, with too little, in too short an amount of time. Instead, it is an opportunity to re-evaluate the priorities, ensure that the critical path issues are addressed in a logical order, and re-organize the team for optimum efficiency. This approach cuts to the marrow of what really matters, and is in that respect *guerrilla* in nature.

Not surprisingly — in the midst of all this turmoil — a new breed of project manager has risen from the ashes of project failure. I call this new breed the Guerrilla Project Manager, and I consider myself among the veterans. To give a voice to this movement, and to provide all of us in the project management community with a point of reference, I have written *Guerrilla Project Management*.

This book is based not only on hard-earned knowledge that I've gleaned from years of experience, but also on industry literature and conversations I've had with other Guerrilla PMs who have rescued (or successfully helmed) a myriad of complex, occasionally white-knuckle projects.

How are Guerrilla PMs different from traditional project managers?

Guerrilla PMs deliberately seek out troubled projects which need to be rescued.

They are the ones you call when the canary is dead, the emperor has no clothes and the bat signal has gone up.

They thrive on the adrenaline rush of making a difference. Most of them started out as traditional project managers, but got knocked out of the ring a few times. They came back swinging, bobbing and weaving, and getting smarter and smarter and about which rules to bend, which ones to break and which ones to invent.

They carry themselves confidently and act swiftly to effect change. Despite this warrior-like vision of a Guerrilla PM, the most successful ones exhibit superior soft skills. That's what wins them the cooperation they need from an often disgruntled set of team members and stakeholders who have probably lost faith in the project.

Although Guerrilla Project Management (GPM) was created as an intervention strategy for troubled IT projects, the principles need not be limited to turnaround situations. GPM is also effective as a tool to prevent chaos, stagnation and waste on normal projects.

Nearly any project which involves cultural change within an organization, high complexity and significant cost should be considered a candidate for GPM methods. Historically, these are the types of projects which are likely to drift into troubled waters. These are the types of projects which tend to meet high-priority and high-risk criteria, justifying GPM from the moment the project launches, not just after it tailspins into trouble.

A Guerrilla project is designed to last no more than 3-12 months. It can be used as a tool to jumpstart major change initiatives, or as a way to expedite the completion of a single project. Although every project (troubled or not) can benefit from the objectives of GPM, there are two types of Guerrilla projects discussed in this book:

- **SWAT Team Turnaround.** Generally reserved for high-priority programs (groups of projects), a SWAT Team Turnaround requires a dedicated team of resources. Led by the Guerrilla PM, the team re-organizes, re-prioritizes and expedites the program. These steps occur in a crisis-intervention mode, meaning that they are handled rapidly and intensively.

- **Basic Turnaround.** A Basic Turnaround is executed under the leadership of a Guerrilla PM, but not necessarily with a team of dedicated resources. A Basic Turnaround is typically appropriate on medium or high-priority projects (as opposed to programs) which meet high-risk criteria.

In both cases, GPM begins with a review of the Guerrilla Justification Criteria. The criteria combine two checklists. One checklist is used to assess the project's priority level, and the other is used to determine its risk profile. The Guerrilla Justification Criteria help you determine whether the project warrants GPM consideration.

Although GPM is designed for IT projects, it is modeled after the crisis-intervention principles of a corporate turnaround. Because IT has become so closely integrated with business strategy, an enterprise perspective is necessary in order for IT projects to succeed.

Why do Most Turnaround Attempts Fail?

As Peter F. Drucker once wrote, "Most turnarounds don't." There are a few basic traps which often ensnare the attempts to recover a troubled project. As mentioned earlier, organizations which have adopted a standardized approach to project recovery tend to experience an overall success rate of almost double those which do not. But few organizations embrace the concept of openly acknowledging—up front—that some projects will hit major roadblocks. Therefore, when they do attempt to rescue a project, they struggle with it in a reactionary and

fearful manner. Listed below are some of the most common reasons that turnaround attempts fail:

- **Reluctance to acknowledge the problems**. To confess that a project will *not* be delivered according to expectations is perhaps the most difficult and politically charged step to be taken in a turnaround situation. No one—not even the most self-assured manager or executive—is eager to admit that a project has run aground under his or her watch. Depending on the criticality and visibility of the project, an admission such as this could potentially jeopardize one's career. It is not surprising, therefore, that the truth about a project's status can become euphemized and obfuscated as it is vetted upward to senior management. Each level wants to believe that it can solve the problem before it becomes visible to the next level. Eventually, this house of cards collapses under its own weight. Nonetheless, the issues facing a troubled project cannot be faced head-on until the stakeholders acknowledge forthrightly that problems do exist.

- **Lack of a true executive owner and champion**. A Guerrilla project needs at least one executive champion who will stand behind the Guerrilla PM, expedite the resolution of high-level roadblocks, and lend his or her inherent authority to the project.

- **Changing the PM without addressing the root causes of the problems**. The objectives for a Guerrilla Project Manager are simple: to seek the truth, stop the bleeding, mitigate the risks, clarify the goals, restore order and forge a pragmatic solution. Often, because the current project manager is beleaguered with historical baggage, this can only be achieved by a new project manager. But new blood alone is not enough. You cannot leapfrog the primary objectives. Unfortunately, most of the time, when new project managers are assigned, they do not have the latitude or the authority to execute on these objectives. Sometimes, by virtue of talent, experience and perseverance, he or she can overcome these limitations. But, in general, they are more likely to run into the same problems faced by the previous project manager.

- **Personal cost is too high for the project manager**. There's no such thing as a timid turnaround. As a Guerrilla PM, you run the risk of over-stepping your boundaries, implying blame, appearing difficult, being perceived as self-aggrandizing and generally jeopardizing the very relationships that you've worked hard to build in the past. Often, it is unrealistic to expect an internal resource to risk his or her relationships to turnaround a project.

- **Lack of a "sense of urgency."** You simply cannot be reactionary in a turnaround situation. You need to leave every meeting with action items, commitments and due dates. If you see something which *might* get in your way later, you need to be all over it like glue. Note the word "urgency"—not "emergency." If you treat too many issues as an emergency, you will lose credibility quickly. Save the emergency card for the things that really matter.

- **Throwing money at a problem.** Henry Ford once said, "Thinking is hard work. That's why so few people do it." Organizations often throw money at an auto-magical solution because they are simply tired of thinking about it themselves. They do this on a prayer that the vendor will be more talented at reducing complexity than they are themselves. This is often an erroneous and expensive assumption which only serves to complicate the problems even more.

- **Too much baggage with the existing team.** There may be interpersonal conflicts. Certain team members may feel as if—no matter what happens—they can't win. They are burned out. That's one of the reasons why—on a SWAT Team Turnaround—the team tends to be composed primarily of outside consultants who have little or no history with the project.

- **Stakeholders have lost interest.** If a project has lacked momentum, it can quickly erode the believability factor among the stakeholders. Also, because business needs change so rapidly, a project's original goals can rapidly become out-of-synch with reality.

- **Artificial deadlines and expectations.** This is also known as the "swift kick" syndrome. This occurs when a frustrated executive issues an edict, demanding certain deliverables at certain times. This measure is used as a substitute for analyzing and addressing the true problems facing the project. As a consequence, the team works overtime in a worried fervor. But little happens. The problems don't get solved. The team feels manipulated. And morale plummets.

- **Fearful team members undermine the efforts.** Guerrilla projects shake up the status quo. Change can intimidate people. Partly, they fear for their jobs. But mostly they fear for a loss of the influence they're familiar with having. Fearful people can undermine the project directly by complaining to their management. But an even more disruptive undermining force is information hoarding, passive-aggressive behavior and a lack of true collaboration.

Why do Guerrilla Projects Succeed?

The number one reason that GPM succeeds whereas most turnaround attempts fail is that GPM is driven entirely with a sense of urgency. On the surface, "a sense of urgency" may sound like a nebulous quality which cannot be taught. It may even sound frenetic, disorganized and short-sighted. In reality, however, a sense of urgency — properly modeled and applied — is none of those things. And remember, on a Guerrilla project, we're talking about *organized* urgency.

It is a simple fact: No project will move forward without a sense of urgency. Without genuine momentum in the form of concrete achievements and deliverables, your project will rap-idly lose the faith and enthusiasm of its stakeholders. Complacency and disengagement will sink in like rigor mortis. And complacency is the death knell for a project.

In my Guerrilla Project Management workshops, I underscore one pervasive theme: *Guerrilla Project Managers must be at war with complacency.* If you are a Guerrilla PM, complacency is the enemy of your project. And the best tool you have to conquer complacency is to model a sense of urgency for your team.

This is where you — as the Guerrilla PM — must walk the walk. You must talk the talk, too, but you cannot pay empty lip service to urgency. A sense of urgency is much more easily demonstrated that it is described.

How Do You Model a Sense of Urgency for Your Team?

Show your team what you expect. Facilitate and demonstrate creative problem solving skills. Acknowledge and reward specific instances of conquering the unknown, identifying obstacles and discovering better ways to tackle the challenges facing your project. Make it obvious that you expect an action plan to occur in each meeting, and that you want to see follow-up and accountability afterwards. An approach like this is a catalyst for progress. As your team experiences momentum, it will begin to develop an organic, self-guided sense of urgency. This is project management Zen. May the force be with you.

In the GPM workshops, we spend a half day or more discussing examples of a sense of urgency and challenging the workshop participants to recall stories from their own backgrounds which illustrate how a sense of urgency (or the lack of it) has impacted their projects in the past. I encourage workshop participants to tell stories about how they *failed* to act urgently, and how they might do it differently now.

Another theme which underscores the GPM workshops is this: *Guerrilla Project Managers must own the unknown.* This means that you are not a victim of the unknown. You do not fear the unknown. Instead, you *own* it. You *own* the responsibility for rapidly discovering and responding to the potential opportunities or hazards which face your project. One of the best tools for this is the Guerrilla Results Initiative (see sidebar on next page).

Beyond a sense of urgency and owning the unknown, there are other fundamental reasons that a Guerrilla project succeeds whereas most turnaround attempts fail. A few of those reasons are listed below:

- **Support from an Executive Champion.** This sounds obvious, yet few projects — even critical projects — are given the executive support that they need to succeed. On a Guerrilla project, you need executive support from a level or two higher than you might expect. The Executive Champion needs some "street cred" in the organization. The Executive Champion cannot only be titular. He or she must attend meetings with the project team at least monthly, communicate with the team in a recurring forum, and deliberately seek ways to move mountains for the project. This is one of the most overlooked opportunities on high-priority projects. Nothing imbues a project team with more belief that the project is important, or more morale that they are doing something important, than the on-going and visible support of an Executive Champion.

- The use of **Guerrilla Results Initiatives** to reduce risk and identify core value quickly. During the Guerrilla Project Management workshops, the participants are shown several examples of Guerrilla Results Initiatives, and challenged to identify ways in which they could have used this approach on projects they have worked on in the past.

- **Emphasis on "Assertive" Analysis.** Cicero, the Roman senator, once wrote: "I would have written you a shorter letter, but I did not have time." On a Guerrilla project, we move rapidly toward the shorter letter. We work to develop the pivotal documentation which drives the project. Too often, projects linger in the doldrums of analysis. On a Guerrilla project, the team members have been trained to identify opportunities to create unique forms of documentation which truly drive the progress of the project. Examples include cross-reference calendars for dependencies, a commitment tracker for follow-up purposes, ramp-up documentation for new team members, and carefully crafted as-is vs. to-be flowcharts.

- **Risks are revealed and addressed quickly.** One of the best tools for this is the Guerrilla Justification Criteria, which include risks that are often overlooked in standard gate reviews or status reports. The underlying theme throughout a Guerrilla project is to monitor and reduce the risks proactively.

- **Requirements Triage ensures that the "main thing is the main thing."** Guerrilla Project Management seeks to deliver tangible value and critical path functionality *first*. Many large projects are complicated by a pork barrel of gold-plated requirements. The Pareto principle applies—80% of the value can be obtained from 20% of the requirements.

- **Commitment to "returning to normal."** A turnaround project can be energizing but also exhausting. Depending on the size of the project (and the depth of its problems), you should not be in Guerrilla mode for more than 3-12 months. After that, it's difficult to sustain enthusiasm. The project needs to be toned down to a dull roar. The team needs some breathing room. Everyone involved will generally be more cooperative if they can see a light at the end of the tunnel, signaling a return to normalcy.

Where do Agile Methodologies Fit on a Guerrilla Project?

The core concepts of Agile methodologies (such as Scrum, XP and RUP) call for close customer involvement, rapid feedback and course adjustment, lean documentation, and development done in short, time-boxed iterations. In general, these are concepts which should be embraced regardless of the type of methodology being used.

However, pure Agile methods require a top-down implementation (that is, management must buy-in, all participants must be trained in Agile, and – if a Project Management Office exists in the organization – its processes must be equipped to accommodate Agile). Unless these steps have already been implemented in an organization, they are difficult to achieve on-the-fly when recovering an important project.

Further, Agile methods, while useful on bug fixes or small enhancements, have not proven to scale well on large projects or programs. From a program management perspective, Agile can be difficult to manage on a broad scope with multiple interdependent systems under construction.

Traditional waterfall methods help to preserve order in a chaotic situation. In the Guerrilla Project Management workshops, we tend to focus on a hybrid approach which preserves the orderliness of waterfall, but also allows for time-boxed iterations during the development phase.

One caveat: On projects for which the end-product is literally being "invented" before your eyes – in other words, the requirements are difficult to lock-down in advance because so much is new – Agile methodologies are critical. But, on projects for which the end-product is relatively simple to envision because it is replacing an existing system, I have found that a simple waterfall approach is the most effective.

Also, on a Guerrilla project, the emphasis is not so much on "lean" documentation, but on "meaningful" documentation – especially the "as-is" vs. "to-be" business processes and IT architecture.

Take the Mystery Out of Estimating

Recommended . . . a book by Steve McConnell called *Software Estimation: Demystifying the Black Art*. The book is excellent and covers a variety of relatively simple estimating techniques. Examples include function points, t-shirt sizing, historical analogies, best and worst case scenarios, and good, old-fashioned professional judgment.

The best estimates – regardless of technique – come from a foundation of detailed granularity. That's what you have to focus on first. How well do you understand the requirements?
How thoroughly have you mapped out the Work Breakdown Structure?

Once we've achieved a certain level of granularity, I ask my teams to choose two estimating techniques from Mr. McConnell's book and cross-check them against each other.

Estimation is not an exact science. However, whenever my teams have used this approach they have produced reasonably accurate, well-supported estimates.

Conquer the Unknowns with Guerrilla Results Initiatives

With Guerrilla Results Initiatives, you glean information about the unknowns, the integration risks and the quality of your assumptions – thus identifying the core value of your project before sending an army after an idea. A Guerrilla Results Initiative is a low-cost, low-risk, expedient way to reveal the dangers that lurk over the next hill. It's a reconnaissance mission designed to capture information which maximizes the value and efficiency of pursing the larger directive. Here's an example on an IT project . . . Let's say that the project calls for delivering 12 new transactions to Production. If possible, structure this so that your team delivers *one* new transaction all the way through to Production *first*. Then, see what you learn from that before tackling the remaining transactions. For an excellent article on this, visit the *Harvard Business Review* on-line and download "Cracking the Code of Change," May/June 2000.

The Ten Commandments for Guerrilla Project Managers

1. **Respect the reality of the stakeholders.** If you're a consultant (as are many Guerrilla PMs), you're just a visitor. The project's stakeholders, however, have a long-term investment in the organization. They possess valued relationships and histories. They will be there long after the turnaround is completed. Your job is to help them succeed gracefully.

2. **Avoid ivory tower treatises.** When compared with formal methodologies, all projects are flawed, period. The stakeholders will only tolerate so much academic acronym slinging before they get impatient. Instead, focus on collaborating with the stakeholders to create an achievable plan.

3. **Ensure that the stakeholders feel "heard."** Listen closely and encourage dialogue. Flatten the lines of communication and seek quick wins to restore morale and boost confidence in the project.

4. **Insist on the support of an Executive Champion.** There must be an Executive Champion, and the Guerrilla PM should report directly to that person. This scenario is critical to preserve the unvarnished truth in status reporting, to secure the confidence of the stakeholders, to expedite important decisions and to remove roadblocks when necessary.

5. **Act quickly and decisively.** You will be wrong sometimes, but GPM enables constant course correction. Momentum is critical toward sustaining enthusiasm on the team and credibility with the stakeholders.

6. **Question the fundamental assumptions first.** Always start with an assessment to ensure that the project's fundamental assumptions are accurate, achievable and worthwhile.

7. **Start with a strong turnaround kickoff speech.** Use this opportunity to assuage fears, set expectations and seek collaboration. Acknowledge that you have no bag of magic tricks,

and that the best results come from collaboration.

8. **Accept the fact that you may be lonely.** You must be an independent, energetic force seemingly impenetrable to criticism or naysayers. The unique social dynamics of a turnaround project require resilience, strong leadership and excellent communication skills.

9. **Be disciplined, but flexible.** Because a turnaround project typically stands outside normal processes, you must have the discipline to act as your own ad hoc PMO.

10. **Empower the team, but make them accountable.** Your role is to set direction. A turnaround project should be an opportunity for the team to shine. Define the problems to be solved and empower the team to invent a solution. If you're doing your job right, they will come back with better ideas than you can imagine.

What's Required of a Guerrilla Project Manager?

The concepts of Guerrilla Project Management (GPM) help lay the foundation for a Guerrilla PM's success. For example, if the project team has been trained in Guerrilla Project Management concepts, and if the Guerrilla PM has the authority he or she needs, and an Executive
Champion stands behind the project, the Guerrilla project itself can operate much like a highly organized military campaign.

Just as in a military battle, however, to succeed the Guerrilla PM must be highly prepared but also flexible. No two battles—and no two turnaround projects—will be exactly alike. As Dwight D. Eisenhower once said, reflecting on his experience as Supreme Commander of the Allied Forces in World War II: "In preparing for battle, I have always found that plans are useless, but planning is indispensable."

Aside from fundamental leadership, the ability to create order out of chaos is a Guerrilla PM's most valuable skill. The Guerrilla PM must transition seamlessly between strategic, directional leadership and hands-on, manage-by-walking-around execution. A Guerrilla PM must be willing to immerse himself in the details to a greater extent than the average project manager, while at the same time coming up for air to sustain a big-picture perspective on the project.

A Guerrilla PM's "Sixth Sense"

You must maintain a sense of urgency, even if you're just exploring new solutions. Hard decisions need to be made fast. And, if you're lucky, you'll have 50-75% of the information you need when you make those decisions. Likewise, a Guerrilla PM's soft skills – such as facilitating dialogue, assuaging fears, coaching team members, inspiring collaboration and setting expectations – will be called upon during a turnaround project to a much greater degree than on a normal project. As a Guerrilla PM, you must have a sixth sense regarding when it's time to stop gathering information and start taking action. At times, it's a tough call to make, especially in the face of high complexity and impatient stakeholders.

The most successful turnarounds—leaving lasting positive results—are executed with a delicate balance of hard and soft approaches. Although there are methodologies for Guerrilla projects (see pages 20-21) do not be deceived by their simplicity. GPM is not a plug-and-play solution. The unique social dynamics of a turnaround project require resilience, strong leadership and excellent communication skills.

Many project managers who herald from traditional, matrixed environments will be relatively unfamiliar with how to wield the level of authority granted to a Guerrilla PM. Further, he or she is likely to be excoriated for minor mistakes which fall into a much harsher light than on a normal project.

On a Guerrilla project, an easy mistake is to communicate too much, too little, too soon or too late. As a Guerrilla PM, you must take hard stances on tough decisions, and you will face resistance in many forms no matter how good you are.

There is a natural tendency, especially among new Guerrilla PMs, to announce plans for a solution too early—before they've had adequate time to assess the issues. We all want to solve problems as quickly as we can, especially when we're charged with turning around a project.

Top 25 Root Causes of IT Project Failure

The causes listed here are based on my own experience, books and industry studies. The causes tend to be ranked differently depending on the source. The causes tend to hunt in packs. Most troubled projects suffer acutely from several of these causes concurrently.

When compared with formally written project management methodologies, all projects are flawed, period. There is no such thing as a perfect environment, process, governance board or project manager. And most projects will face challenges politically in one shape or another.

A project manager must be prepared to act as an ad-hoc PMO, exerting discipline in areas which might be lacking within the organization (such as requirements, testing, estimating, risk management or change control). A strong project manager can usually succeed despite the limitations, regardless of methodology or oversight. Still, even the strongest project manager will occasionally face problems which are simply outside of his or her control, and can only be addressed with executive intervention.

The causes listed here are the subject of fervent dialogue during Guerrilla Project Management workshops. It can be argued that some of the causes are root-level, while others are more symptomatic. I agree. Still, entire books (or at least chapters of books) have been dedicated to the discussion of many of these issues individually.

Quick, Powerful Advice on Rescuing Troubled IT Projects

I have listed what I consider to be the top ten causes at the top of the list. In general, based on my research, experience and feedback from workshop participants, I believe the top ten to be accurately ranked.

1. Inadequate rigor surrounding the estimating process
2. Poor match of resources to roles
3. Project team lacks understanding of business processes (that is, the team does not understand the as-is business processes, or the ways in which the system under construction will change those processes)
4. Lack of an executive champion who stands behind the team
5. Unclear business objectives (big budgets may have been allocated, yet there could be minimal or non-existent blueprints for the future)
6. Inadequate user involvement during design and construction
7. Lack of momentum causes project to flame-out, resources gradually get re-assigned, stakeholders lose interest, business need is obsoleted or handled another way
8. Poorly written or incomplete requirements
9. Failure to organize the project into manageable chunks (this is a complexity risk)
10. Lack of change management (can lead to scope creep, mis-aligned expectations, problems with overall software and infrastructure compatibility issues)
11. Challenges with vendor management (could be complicated by multi-tiered vendors, a "no turning back now" dilemma, or poorly defined expectations)
12. Lack of project management processes
13. Organization is simply trying to do too much at once (priorities compete, dependencies between projects collide, credibility erodes, enthusiasm wanes)
14. Weak project manager (could lack project management skills, business knowledge, leadership, communication skills or a sense of urgency)
15. Lack of a software development methodology
16. Lack of risk management (dependency tracking, follow-up, awareness of red flags)
17. Failure to track and respond to basic metrics impacting the project (scope, schedule, budget, velocity, ROI)
18. Poor communication (weak status reporting, fear of telling the truth, failure to align expectations regarding scope, schedule, cost and quality)
19. Project may be larger in scope than the organization has attempted in the past
20. Project may use tools which are new to the organization
21. Inadequate time and planning allocated to testing
22. Failure to trace requirements through design, testing and delivery
23. Data quality problems (multiple disparate systems, difficult to map data elements)
24. Browbeating, unrealistic expectations and the blame game have damaged morale
25. Inadequate tools for requirements management, testing, source code management and change control

The Guerrilla Justification Criteria

M ost projects for which GPM is a logical choice meet two basic criteria: They are high-priority *and* high-risk. I have also been asked, occasionally, to implement a scaled-down version of GPM on lower-priority projects which have simply stagnated indefinitely (I call these Basic Turnarounds).

GPM often involves outside intervention, an added cost in the form of a Guerrilla PM and a dedicated SWAT Team, and a temporary cultural adjustment within the organization. Therefore, GPM is generally reserved for high-priority projects, in which the outcome of the project would have a significant impact on the organization's profitability, market value, ability to compete, or ability to do business.

To determine if a project is high risk involves the analysis of hard and soft data. For example, hard data would indicate that the project has clearly not met expectations for scope, budget, schedule or quality. The analysis of soft data, however, requires some degree of managerial instinct and awareness. For example, if the project team's morale has plummeted, that's a soft indication that the project is in trouble. Likewise, the project may lack clarity, direction and leadership—again, those are soft data points, although hard to accept when the project fails.

To help assess a project's priority level and its risk level, I have provided the Guerrilla Justification Criteria. These criteria are provided as a basic guide, which I have found useful when helping my clients to assess the priority and risk level of the project.

Guerrilla Justification Criteria: PRIORITY Analysis Statements

Preface each statement with "Project failure would cause . . ." (check the relevant statements)

1. A glaring write-off on the financial statement
2. Inability to collect a large receivable
3. High risk of fines (or potential loss of licensure or eligibility) from a regulatory agency
4. Spotlight of scrutiny from executives, the board, shareholders or Wall Street
5. Loss or compromise of an important customer relationship
6. Potential for costly lawsuits
7. Potential termination of key leaders in the organization
8. Inability to deliver an essential business function
9. Inability to execute other projects or functions
   which depend on the successful completion of this one
10. Loss of a clear opportunity to gain profit
11. Clear loss of a competitive or decisive marketing advantage
12. Potential reduction in the market value of the company
13. Other: Unique reasons that this project is important

Guerrilla Justification Criteria: RISK Analysis Questions

Check the questions which seem relevant to the project under consideration:

1. Have reasonable deadlines for phase deliverables (requirements, design, code, testing, implementation) been missed?
2. Is there a detailed Work Breakdown Structure (WBS) supporting the project? If so, is it clear? Have tasks been broken down in to sufficient granularity (no more than 10 days each)? Have task dependencies been tracked within the WBS?
3. Is it difficult to get a clear answer about the status of the project or the root causes of its problems? Are people hiding? Note: Silence is the first sign of trouble.
4. Is your organization equipped to deliver the project successfully (adequate experience and availability of resources)?
5. Does the project's scope include requirements from multiple departments and/or dependencies on other projects, making it inherently more complex?
6. Are the goals clear? Can you describe the project's purpose in a few sentences?
7. Because of frustration on the project, has the organization experienced (or is it likely to experience) an exodus of valuable knowledge resources?
8. Has the project been granted additional time and/or money more than once?
9. Has the scope of the project expanded significantly? If so, have estimates been provided to assess the impact on the project's resources, schedule and cost?
10. How fresh are the requirements? Are the requirements well-written and complete? If the requirements are more than six months old, have they been reviewed by the stakeholders to ensure their relevance?
11. Are there complaints from the customer about quality, cost or timeliness?
12. Has the project lingered in the "90% complete" stage for more than two months?
13. Has there been significant turnover in project managers?
14. Is there an Executive Champion for this project?
15. Does this project suffer from a chronic lack of urgency?
16. Is the project larger in scope than your organization is familiar with handling?
17. Does the project involve technology which is relatively new to the project team?
18. Is there a healthy, positive relationship with the key vendor(s) on this project?
19. Was there a disciplined process used to create the estimates?

Einstein once wrote: "Not everything that can be counted counts. And not everything that counts can be counted." There is no mathematical formula to assess the items that you've checked or noted above. The purpose of the Guerrilla Justification Criteria is to stimulate your own managerial intuition – to help you assess the things which count but cannot be counted.

Based on what you've checked, do you *believe* that the project under consideration is high-priority and/or a high-risk? If yes, refer to the flowcharts on the next two pages to determine if the project warrants a Basic Turnaround or a SWAT Team Turnaround.

Flowchart for a Basic Turnaround

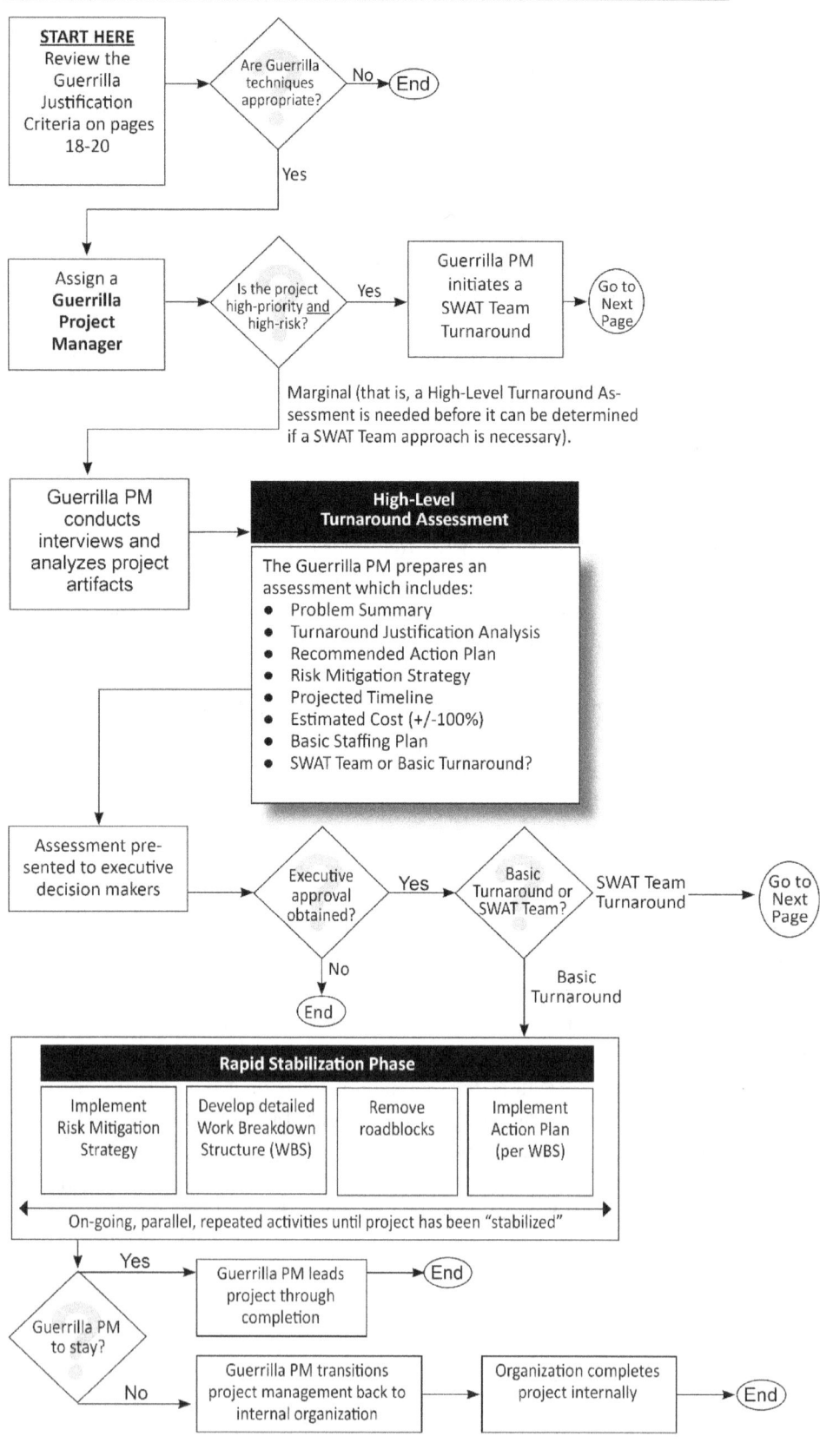

Flowchart for a SWAT Team Turnaround

After confirming that a SWAT Team Turnaround is justified, start here . . .

Priorities =
Protect the organization's interests. Stop "throwing good money after bad." Buy time to think.

1. Stop the Bleeding
(occurs mostly behind the scenes)

- Meet with executive stakeholders to discuss high-level action plan
- Ensure that code base, project documentation and hardware are in a secured location
- Identify essential team members and meet with them individually to prevent a knowledge exodus
- Determine if any work should be stopped immediately (due to cost and/or directional uncertainty)
- Consider freezing payments or financial commitments temporarily (especially if vendor management issues need to be resolved)
- Assess damage control and high-level risk mitigation

Priorities =
Discover the "true status" of the project. Act swiftly to restore clarity and direction.

2. Conduct Assertive Analysis Phase

- Organize and recruit SWAT team
- Ensure that the "as-is" process flows have been carefully diagrammed
- **Declare Amnesty**: Encourage the freedom to ask the right questions, answer boldy and think creatively
- Facilitate a Requirements Triage (use multiple, day-long sessions if necessary)
- Diagram the "to be" process flows (after Requirements Triage)
- Prepare Project Plan (scope, charter, approach, known risks, timeline, etc.)
- Develop high-level Work Breakdown Structure for delivery of critical path milestones and high-priority functionality

3. Develop Detailed Turnaround Plan

- Executive summary of project plan and recommended "next steps"
- Cost estimates (+/- 25%)
- Project timeline and milestones
- Resource Allocation Plan
- SWAT Team Organizational Chart
- Risk Mitigation Strategy
- Turnaround Justification Analysis (Does it still make sense for this project to continue?)
- High-Level Transition Plan: How will this project eventually be transitioned "back to normal"?
- Seek Executive approval and commitment for Detailed Turnaround Plan . . .

Executive approval obtained? — No → (End)

Priorities =
Deliver critical path milestones and high-priority functionality.

4. Implement Rapid Execution Phase

- Conduct daily SWAT Team Status Meetings
- Encourage flexibility to "fail fast," evaluate results, and adjust course
- Constantly update a highly refined Work Breakdown Structure (WBS), organizing tasks in taks which are no longer than 1-3 days duration
- Work side-by-side with end-users to build a proof of concept
- Establish a consistent Communications Plan to reduce stakeholder "worry" factor
- Develop an Implementation Plan (start early with the "end in mind")
- Remove roadblocks which interfere with critical path milestones

Priority =
Empower the organization to move forward with the project "in good health."

5. Transition the Project "Back to Normal"

- Develop a Detailed Transition Plan
- Update project documentation to reflect "reality" of completed project
- Ensure that adequate training and/or user documentation has been planned or provided
- Summarize any "dependencies" between this project and others
- Document known "defects" and "workarounds"
- Capture "lessons learned" in post-mortem
- Conduct formal "hand-off" meeting

(End)

Description of Guerrilla Project Management Deliverables

Basic Turnaround
(see flowchart on page 20)

Description of a Basic Turnaround

A Basic Turnaround is appropriate for projects which are deemed to be a "medium" risk or priority based on a review of the Guerrilla Justification Criteria. On a Basic Turnaround, there is no SWAT Team. Depending on the complexity of the project, the Guerrilla PM may work alone (or perhaps with one or two consulting analysts) to conduct interviews, study the status of the project and prepare a High-Level Turnaround Assessment.

Upon delivery of the Assessment, an executive review is required to agree on the next steps. Generally, those steps could be one of the following:

- Move forward on the project with a few basic changes to improve its chances of success. In this case, the project can probably be delivered internally without the assistance of a Guerrilla PM.
- Continue with a Basic Turnaround, with a Guerrilla PM, moving to the next step: the Rapid Stabilization Phase.
- Launch a SWAT Team Turnaround, in which a dedicated team of consultants is installed to deliver the project rapidly.
- Kill the project entirely.
- Retain a few objectives of the project, but fold them into another project where the fit seems appropriate.

Content of a High-Level Turnaround Assessment

- Problem Summary
- Description of Primary Roadblocks
- Recommended Action Plan (See options listed above)
- Risk Mitigation Strategy
- Basic Staffing Plan
- Projected Timeline
- Estimated Cost (+/-100%)

Advantages of a Basic Turnaround

- A Basic Turnaround is less intrusive than a SWAT Team Turnaround, and therefore involves less of a culture shock.
- There is less up-front cost.
- On smaller projects (excluding programs, which include multiple projects), the High-Level Turnaround Assessment may indicate that the roadblocks facing the project are simple to resolve — thus negating the need for a Guerrilla PM or a SWAT Team.

Disadvantages of a Basic Turnaround

Loss of momentum. The High-Level Turnaround Assessment may indicate that a SWAT Team Turnaround is necessary in order to execute the recovery. If this is the case, the organization will have lost 30-60 days of time which could have been used for setting up the SWAT Team and gathering more detailed information.

Timeframe for a Basic Turnaround

A High-Level Turnaround Assessment typically requires 30-60 days to complete, depending on the complexity of the project. The deliverables after the High-Level Turnaround Assessment (assuming that the executives choose to move forward) are typically delivered in 3-6 months.

SWAT Team Turnaround
(see flowchart on page 21)

Description of a SWAT Team Turnaround

A SWAT Team Turnaround is appropriate for larger projects or programs which are deemed to be high-risk and high-priority, based on a review of the Guerrilla Justification Criteria. The process for implementing a SWAT Team Turnaround is more sophisticated and politically sensitive than that of a Basic Turnaround. The fundamental deliverable of a SWAT Team Turnaround is the Detailed Turnaround Plan, followed then by delivering the project itself.

There are two phases of a SWAT Team Turnaround which occur before the development of the Detailed Turnaround Plan. Those phases are:

- Stop the Bleeding. The primary objectives of this phase are to protect the organization's interests, stop throwing good money after bad and buy time to think. Certain parts of the project may be suspended temporarily in this phase.
- Assertive Analysis. The primary objectives of this phase are to discover the true status of the project and act swiftly to restore clarity and direction. There is an emphasis on "assertive" because many projects fall victim to the doldrums of analysis.

Upon delivery of the Detailed Turnaround Plan, an executive review is required to agree upon the next steps. The choices to be made are comparable to the Basic Turnaround (see left). But the conditions are different because a SWAT Team Turnaround is typically focused on a much larger, more critical project or program than a Basic Turnaround.

Content of a Detailed Turnaround Plan

- Executive Summary (Defines the project. Describes what has been done so far. Describes the basic problems discovered. Describes the recommended action plan.)

- Turnaround Justification Analysis (Should we move forward? If so, how and why? Where is the core value of the project?)
- Cost estimates (+/- 50%).
- Project timeline and milestones.
- Detailed Work Breakdown Structure.
- Resource Allocation Plan (estimated hours, types of resources, where we'll find the people).
- SWAT Team Organizational Chart. Note: Many of the SWAT Team members will already be in place by the time the Detailed Turnaround Plan is presented.
- Risk Mitigation Strategy.
- Revised Requirements (based on a Requirements Triage, which is conducted during the Assertive Analysis Phase).
- High-Level Transition Plan. (How will this project eventually be transitioned back to normal so that a SWAT Team is no longer necessary?).

Advantages of a SWAT Team Turnaround

- On large, high-priority/high-risk projects or programs, a SWAT Team Turnaround assures the best chance of success.
- The Detailed Turnaround Plan provides an in-depth look at the truth and represents a relatively turn-key solution.
- There's a strong leave-behind value because your organization's employees will witness and participate in the comprehensive planning phase of a SWAT Team Turnaround.

Disadvantages of a SWAT Team Turnaround

- Temporary culture shock in the organization. This can be softened in many ways by a skillful Guerrilla PM. Nonetheless, there will always be an initial period of discomfort and doubt among your employees. Throughout this book , you will see multiple references to the success factors of a turnaround project.
- A SWAT Team Turnaround requires an investment in consultants. You must weigh this against the criticality and benefits of the project or program itself. The cost is usually negligible when compared with project failure.

Timeframe for a SWAT Team Turnaround

A Detailed Turnaround Plan typically requires 3-4 months to complete, depending on the complexity of the project. The deliverables after the Detailed Turnaround Plan is presented (assuming that the executives choose to move forward), are prioritized based on critical path analysis and typically delivered in phases of 3-4 months each.

Five Critical Success Factors for Guerrilla Project Managers

Critical Success Factor #1:
Start Right with an Executive Champion

My advice to people who want to manage Guerrilla projects within their own organization is this: Get senior management to ask you for a turnaround assessment. Never present it out of the blue. Let them warm up to the possibility. And let them give you important information before you write or distribute the plan. Regardless of whether they ordain you to lead the turnaround, you will have earned the respect of your colleagues by handling it with a deft sense of corporate politics and a respect for the careers and motivations of the stakeholders.

Further, I would advise never to attempt a turnaround unless you are supported by a respected Executive Champion who can help you navigate potentially treacherous waters. As Teddy Roosevelt once said regarding foreign policy, "Walk softly, but carry a big stick."

Because GPM represents a significant departure from traditional methodology, it must be implemented as a directive from senior management.

While a traditional project needs an owner, a Guerrilla project requires a greater degree of ownership in the form of an Executive Champion. On a Guerrilla project, the Executive Champion performs several important roles, such as:

- Serving as the primary point of contact for other executives who may be affected by the results of the project
- Providing encouragement to the project team by dropping in occasionally on team meetings to voice his or her support
- Expediting bureaucratic roadblocks when necessary
- Seeking assistance from other departments when the project generates special requests
- Securing and authorizing the financing for the project
- Assuring that the Guerrilla PM performs according to plan

If you are a senior executive responsible for assigning the Executive Champion role to someone, consider choosing one of your best and brightest executives—someone with a lot of "street cred" in the organization. If you think a manager can handle it, consider assigning the role to an executive or VP instead. The likelihood of success for your project increases exponentially based on the clout and skill of the Executive Champion.

Ideally, the Guerrilla PM will report directly to the Executive Champion, thus providing the authority needed by the Guerrilla PM to execute the project. When an executive authorizes a Guerrilla project, he or she has launched a highly visible leadership initiative. The tenacity, momentum and results of a Guerrilla project will reflect positively on everyone involved.

Critical Success Factor #2:
Take the Pain Early

In GPM, a Requirements Triage is incorporated early in the process. The triage must be conducted rapidly and intensively, often in multiple day-long sessions. To de-scope requirements gradually is like cutting off a piece of your arm one inch at a time. With each reduction in scope, you risk upsetting the expectations of the stakeholders. It's best to take this pain early and quickly, while the stakeholders are psychologically receptive to negotiating.

The purpose of the Requirements Triage is not only to set expectations, but also to lay the foundation for a Detailed Turnaround Plan. The triage is not always necessary for a Basic Turnaround, but on a SWAT Team Turnaround—in which a broader scope of requirements is usually involved—it is essential to conduct the Requirements Triage early in the process.

Critical Success Factor #3:
Organize Your Team Wisely

On one project, I agreed to inherit the team "as is" when I took over using Guerrilla Project Management. Frankly, that was a mistake because the project needed some fresh perspectives, which is often the case on turnaround projects. Because the project had endured 18 months of brutal corporate politics, certain team members had been severely battle-scarred. Their skepticism and resistance impeded progress on the project. Their negativity caused discomfort for the entire team. It also undermined the team's and our own credibility.

Ironically, each of the problematic team members was highly capable and competent. They were simply worn out and had lost interest in the success of the project.

On a Guerrilla project, the choices you make on how to staff your SWAT Team are fundamental to the success of the project. Further, the Guerrilla PM must have the flexibility to remove, replace or re-assign team members during the turnaround. Today, before I start a Guerrilla project, I ensure that the client is aware that changes within the team will be an on-going possibility.

One warning signal . . . watch out for knowledge-hoarders, that is, people who are clinging to their jobs by virtue of their domain knowledge. Do not be lured in by the "holy cow" syndrome. This can be poisonous for the team. Other team members resent it. It is not healthy for a project or an enterprise to be held hostage by individual knowledge resources.

Ideally, you should map out the specific types of domain knowledge needed on the project (that is, business processes and familiarity with the application code and data models) and then verify that the team has at least two developers and two business analysts in each area who can step in for each other whenever necessary.

Sometimes, a team member's positive attitude is more important than his or her knowledge and experience—even on a tight deadline. It is erroneous to assume that knowledge resources simply cannot be replaced. It's amazing how quickly a smart resource with a positive attitude can adapt to a new project and figure out what needs to be done.

On a Guerrilla project, I am emphatic about creating detailed process flows which represent the as-is and to-be environments. This documentation enables an expedited ramp-up of new team members. It also imposes clarity on the project. An additional measure I try to take is to pair-up resources so that there is always safety in the redundancy.

Are you a Tigger or an Eeyore?

"Tiggers bound with enthusiasm, optimism and a willingness to change, to try new things. Eyeores are victims and complainers and lack responsibility for driving change. They can be deceivingly intelligent and thorough, but their negativity can easily drag down an entire group of people. They can be passive-aggressive, behaving as if they are on board, when in reality they are undermining the mission, the leadership or the work of others. If you hire Eyeores, you will have a harder time getting the Tiggers to join you. And you desperately need the Tiggers. The Tiggers are attracted to each other, as are the Eyeores."

- Mindy Grossman, CEO of Home Shopping Network, as quoted in the *Wall Street Journal*, 2009

Critical Success Factor #4:
Go to the Scene

On one project, I had five testers dedicated to the team. For the first three months, I simply took their word for anything they said. If they told me they needed eight hours to test a piece of functionality, or that something did not work, or that something did work, we graciously accepted this as gospel because they were—after all—the technical experts. Then we lost two testers and the timeline was compressed. So, I decided to jump in and learn how to test the system myself. This took us about two weeks. Wow, what an eye-opener . . .

Because of the extra step I took (which would normally be considered outside the purview of the project manager), I suddenly understood what the testers were talking about. It became clear to me that the entire approach we were taking to testing the system was fundamentally flawed. I realized that there was a chasm between a developer's interpretation of what worked and an end-user's interpretation of what worked. I also discovered that our testers were jaded and determined to find fault with the vendor's work.

Because of this experience, I drove a Testing Priority Triage which was probably the single-most progressive step we took on the project. Further, because of our fresh perspective on the project, we noticed several pieces of functionality which were either unnecessary or so poorly conceived that they should have been eliminated. This led to the gradual de-scoping of certain requirements.

My point is this: As a Guerrilla PM, there are huge leaps to be made if you dive-in to understand the functionality of the system that your team is developing. It does not matter if you are a technical expert. What does matter is that small details can lead to big discoveries. So, push for understanding. Ask more questions. Study the process flows and keep them updated. Seek a hands-on learning experience. Inevitably, you will find that this process leads to changes in your strategy for leading the project. Further, you will earn the respect of your team and your executive sponsors.

Critical Success Factor #5:
Be There as a Leader, Not as an Administrator

Properly managed, a Guerrilla project moves forward rapidly. As a consequence, certain pieces of project documentation may fail to keep pace with changes on the project. On one project, for example, we worked diligently to ensure that the documentation was updated. However, because we were in turnaround mode—and most of the documentation revolved around the organization's standard process—we found ourselves force-fitting standardized documentation into a largely non-standard process. As a result, the documentation did not effectively represent reality.

Likewise, there were all sorts of subtleties regarding how to keep a project in green status on the executive dashboard. A project manager could easily spend half of his or her time working the system and the other half managing the project.

Although the documentation was necessary from a corporate standards perspective, in our case—for that particular project—it did nothing to move the project forward. This was an unnecessary stressor in the midst of managing a project in crisis. Today—because I work in new environments frequently—I must strike a balance between respect for the organization's standard processes and terminology, and a determination to show results on the project.

If my client's organization has a well-rooted, familiar way of doing certain things (such as obtaining budgetary approval, logging time, change control, status reporting, etc.), I often request the support of a project administrator from within the client's organization.

Misconceptions about Guerrilla Projects

Certain misconceptions exist about the nature of Guerrilla projects. For example, Guerrilla PMs are generally more positively received than one might expect. By the time a Guerrilla PM is hired, the general feeling among team members is that the project is in almost total disarray and needs strong leadership.

Guerrilla PMs are especially well-received when they are clearly endorsed by senior management. Further, because a Guerrilla PM has no personal history on the project, he or she begins with a temporary honeymoon. This does not last long, but there are a number of important tasks which can and should be accomplished during this period. One example of this is the Requirements Triage, in which the core value of the project is re-considered, re-documented and re-prioritized.

A second misconception is that a Guerrilla project is extremely stressful. This need not be true. There are certain conditions and expectations that must be agreed upon before a turnaround is executed; however, if those conditions are met—and you've hired an experienced Guerrilla PM—the turnaround itself will probably be much less stressful than the project was prior to the turnaround.

However, the high-stress misconception is also rooted in fact because most software project turnarounds are neither organized nor executed in a Guerrilla manner. A common example of this is to replace the project manager but to change nothing about the fundamentally flawed assumptions and structure of the project.

Unfortunately, we as human beings tend to resist and deny what we need the most. This fact is compounded on a project level in the workplace where we all strive to protect the careers and reputations that we've worked hard to earn. Because of this, while I am often called upon to rescue a project, in reality—most of the time — I am turning around a turnaround.

Another misconception about turnarounds is that they are an opportunity for heroics—that a Guerrilla PM is necessarily driven by the white knight syndrome. You learn quickly in this business that—no matter how strong a leader you are—you are almost completely at the mercy of the expertise, initiative and attitude of your team.

As Will Rogers once said, "Being a hero is about the shortest lived profession on Earth." You are likely to be forgotten soon after you leave the project. Ideally, you will have left something behind which benefits the company, its employees and its shareholders.

Another misconception is the command-and-control assumption about the Guerrilla PM's role. Indeed, it is true that during the initial stages of a turnaround, you don't have much time for democracy. But after order has been imposed on the situation—and assuming that you have selected your team carefully—you should find yourself collaborating more than giving orders. Therefore, your real challenge as the Guerrilla PM is to ensure that your team members feel included, appreciated and inspired. Nonetheless, your team will look to you for a strong sense of direction—which is much more important than any given order.

Should a Project be Shut-Down Pending the Results of an Assessment?

Most of the time, if a client calls me seeking to recover a troubled project, that client is already saying, "This project is important to us and we want to see it succeed." In other words, they don't want to *stop* the project — not yet anyway. They've accepted the fact that the project is not running efficiently, and that significant measures will need to be taken to revive it. They've accepted the fact that time and money are being wasted.

Nonetheless, they do not have the luxury of simply shutting down and starting over. They've probably already obtained funding (which can be a long, grueling process in itself). They've probably already staffed up a project team, and they are afraid to let people go for fear of not being able to get them back. And, they do not want to be associated with a project which had to be "shut down" – to them, that's an admission of failure.

In my early days of turnaround work, when assessing troubled projects, I found myself tyrannized with a nagging thought in the back of my mind: "I wish I could just start this project over and do it right from the beginning." After all, what's done is done, and it's all a sunk cost up to this point – right?

Well, that was the idealist in me. Out of necessity, the pragmatist won out. Today, I rarely propose a complete "scrap and re-do." Instead, I focus on the positives, and try to leverage that to obtain consensus on the improvements which need to be made to succeed with the project as a whole.

I am reminded of a quote from Teddy Roosevelt, whom I consider to be one of the most effective executives of the 20th century: "Do what you can, with what you have, where you are."

While your assessment may recommend bold actions, the words "start over" are not likely to be well-received in an executive briefing.

Another reason to keep the project alive is so that you can clearly observe the project's problems in stark relief. Further, the turnaround assessment process involves conducting interviews with team members. They are much more likely to provide you with useful insights if the project is still in flight. Also, after a turnaround plan has been agreed upon, the project team will be more receptive and cooperative if they feel that they have been heard and given a fair shake. Shutting down the project abruptly could offend them unnecessarily.

All this said, I have certainly seen occasions in which parts of the project needed to be stopped immediately. This was usually because of unclear business objectives, understaffing, inappropriate combinations of projects, or simply illogical prioritization – not necessarily because of a poorly performing team. In these cases, when the issues are plain as daylight, I've generally met with little resistance in recommending postponement or cessation of activity. In fact, it is usually perceived as a relief.

What Does It Mean to "Return to Normal"?

A Guerrilla project is a highly visible initiative in the spotlight of senior-level attention and awareness. A Guerrilla project often pulls some people away from their regular jobs and into an intense push to design new processes, build new databases and applications, and to complete the test-and-fix loop. A Guerrilla project is oriented toward standing up the highest priority requirements as quickly as possible, thus laying the foundation for the success of the remainder of the project which will probably *not* be executed in Guerrilla mode.

On a Guerrilla project, you are likely to modify some of the formalities such as detailed documentation and gate reviews that might be standard practice in your organization. The concepts of Guerrilla Project Management are designed to impose a sense of order on the process, but the underlying theme of Guerrilla Project Management is a sense of urgency, relentless prioritization and a concerted push toward a well-defined set of goals.

A Guerrilla project can be energizing and exciting, but it can also be exhausting. In general, you cannot expect a team to remain in Guerrilla mode for more than 3-12 months, depending on the scope of the project. Go any longer than that, and you risk burn-out. People cannot live like that forever. They have to see an end in sight. They have to believe that they are working toward a finite goal, upon which life may return to normal.

That's why it's important to clearly define the goals of the Guerrilla project. And, upon achievement of those goals, when the stakeholders are feeling more confident about the project, it's time to celebrate. Not just a happy hour, but a genuine team builder. For example, in one organization, the senior management dressed in waiter outfits, took orders, and delivered meals and drinks to the team members. During the team builder, it's important for the senior leadership to give short speeches to highlight the accomplishments. It's also important to thank individuals out loud, and to describe the importance of their specific contributions.

As a rule, on a Guerrilla project, you do not want to go more than six months without a team builder like this. Also, as a rule, you don't want to run the secondary phases of the project (if applicable) in Guerrilla mode. You may need to single out certain high-risk areas in the secondary phases for Guerrilla management, but your team is likely to mutiny on you if they think an entire 2-4 year enterprise initiative is going to operate at a Guerrilla pace.

The team builder is also an opportunity to explain what a "return to normal" will entail. Perhaps the project will return to the umbrella of the organization's PMO (if applicable). Perhaps some consultants will be departing the project, and maybe some permanent employees can return full-time to their normal jobs. It may be possible to reduce the frequency of the status meetings, or to have less hands-on involvement from senior management. Whatever you're changing, call attention to it. Don't miss this opportunity to make it feel authentic to the team.

In general, however, you must walk a fine line between holding a victory dance and preparing the organization for the secondary phases of the project (again, if applicable). You don't want to lose momentum or trigger complacency. But you do want to acknowledge the stress they've endured. One thing about the team builder: Do not treat it as an opportunity to talk about goals for the next phases of the project. Let the people breathe.

Understanding Business Processes – a Great Way to Boost the Morale on Your Team and to Reassure the Stakeholders

On a large, complex re-engineering project, your best friend is a set of extremely well-designed "as-is" vs. "to-be" diagrams, and a graphic timeline of release dates and dependencies. It's best to use a consistent format for these diagrams, and to make them available on a broad and granular levels. Not only is this a useful training tool as you ramp-up new team members, but it also serves to convince the stakeholders that you understand the business and you know what you're doing. It's hard work to create these diagrams, but the payoff is big. Depending on the size, complexity and duration of your project, you will find yourself updating them and re-using them often in a variety of presentations. The diagrams will also enable you to manage multiple project managers and teams effectively. In fact, these diagrams can be an empowering morale booster. Why? Because everyone likes to know where his or her part of the project fits into the overall vision.

How Will Employees Respond to Guerrilla Project Management?

Properly led, the GPM objectives should be well-communicated to the affected stakeholders and existing team members. The key to ensuring a positive response is to carefully control the expectations of the group. To do this, you must be prepared to educate the group on how GPM works, who will be implementing it, the timeline and the challenges you expect to face.

The implementation of GPM involves frequent status meetings and tasks which are sometimes organized into chunks of a few days – not weeks or months. This level of scrutiny and managerial involvement will be foreign to most of your employees. While they may chafe under this scrutiny at first, the forward momentum of a GPM project often ameliorates their discomfort.

Initially, your employees—especially those who have been assigned to the SWAT Team—will fall into two distinct camps: 1) The Doubters, and 2) The Believers.

The Doubters will warn you about the way things have been done in the past. This is valuable, especially when you are assembling as-is process flows (one secret to the remarkable progress which can be achieved on a GPM project). The Doubters will keep you honest. Respect them, listen to them and work with them. Eventually, you will earn their confidence.

The Believers, on the other hand, will be enthusiastic contributors to the to-be process flows. They will enjoy the Guerrilla project because it circumvents the organization's standard bureaucracy—thus freeing the path for rapid implementation. The Believers boost the morale of the project team. However, they must be handled with care because they will inevitably—in their optimism—encounter cultural roadblocks which frustrate them.

Before implementing GPM, one common concern is that the organization will withstand a sudden knowledge exodus of the most essential team members. If GPM is followed closely, however, those members will have already been consulted and reassured of their roles before the turnaround kickoff meeting is held.

When is Guerrilla Project Management *Not* Necessary?

The fact that a project is troubled does not necessarily imply that it is an appropriate candidate for GPM. The Guerrilla Justification Criteria are designed to help you make this determination early in the process. Here are some possible reasons that GPM might not be appropriate:

- Upon closer analysis, it may be determined that the project is facing an unforeseen roadblock which can be eradicated. In this case, measures would be taken to remove the roadblock and to adjust the project plan accordingly.
- Sometimes, simple rousing (based on the possibility of launching a turnaround) is enough to revitalize the project. The best stimulus for this revitalization is to define specific problems and invite the team to recommend solid solutions.
- It's not easy to find someone with the talent, skill set and willingness needed in a Guerrilla PM. And, those who possess this skill set tend to either be booked or reserve themselves for projects which meet certain conditions. Therefore, if you attempt to implement GPM without an experienced Guerrilla PM, you have essentially created another risk for an already-troubled project.
- The project may not be critical enough to justify GPM. While it may take longer to fix the project using standard methodology, the organization could decide to absorb this risk.

Who Should Be On the SWAT Team?

This is one of the most important questions on a turnaround project. The design of your turnaround project's organizational chart warrants careful consideration. While there are certain consistent roles that belong on nearly every SWAT Team (such as developers, data architects, analysts, technical writers, requirements facilitators and test leads), there are many issues to consider when selecting the people who will fill those roles. Here are a few of those issues:

- How large is the project? Is it actually multiple projects within a program? If so, the Guerrilla PM will probably be leading project managers instead of managing the technical resources directly.
- Who are the indispensable knowledge resources? This includes both technical and non-technical subject matter experts. Is the organization willing to dedicate these resources to the project? What is the attitude of these resources? Note: The positive momentum of GPM can usually win-over resources who have suffered from the inevitable pain and frustration of a troubled project. However, when building your team, you must ask: "Is this person's attitude too far gone? Can it be redeemed?"
- What are the financial resources available to staff the SWAT Team? Is the organization receptive to hiring outside consultants who will be available only for the life of the project?

A Guerrilla project is more likely to succeed if the team is composed primarily of external consultants who have experienced the turnaround mentality on past projects. This is not a reflection of the competence level of the permanent employees. Instead, it is a factor of the inherent differences in circumstance between consultants and permanent employees. Here are a few advantages that consultants bring to a turnaround project:

- They bring a fresh perspective because they have no personal baggage from the project's history.
- For the tougher decisions which must be made on a Guerrilla project (such as re-organizing the team, exercising relentless prioritization on the requirements, and re-estimating the project), there will be less potential residual animosity if the Guerrilla PM is an outside consulting resource.
- They have no agendas or turfs to protect. They are relatively immune to corporate politics.
- Ideally, they will have worked with the Guerrilla PM in the past. This enables them to communicate in shorthand with the Guerrilla PM, who often has specific ideas and standards for the project deliverables he or she wants produced.
- Selected properly, they are often among the top ten percent of performers in their fields. They bring that something extra of star players such as strong initiative, insight, experience and problem-solving skills.

- They are less fearful about speaking their minds. This is different from most permanent employees who must always live with a certain fear factor, asking themselves: "How much am I willing to risk by expressing the truth?"
- Especially on large enterprise change initiatives, you need project managers who boldly "own the unknown," and operate with an innate "sense of urgency." These are not easy qualities to screen for in the hiring process. However, if you have project managers on the team who do *not* exhibit these qualities, a large change initiative is likely to eat them alive. As the Guerrilla PM driving the initiative, you *must* have the flexibility to re-organize the team however you deem appropriate. You *must* have the flexibility to get the right people on the bus in the right roles. Your flexibility in this regard is much higher if the team is composed primarily of contractors, otherwise you can face formidable HR-related delays and roadblocks.

How Can Executives Help Prevent Troubled Projects?

The formal answer to this question—the answer you'll hear from the project management gurus and various IT standards organizations—is that you need to establish a Project Management Office, a governance board and a development methodology to support your organization. Theoretically, if you do these things, and you progressively evolve into higher levels of maturity, you will reduce the likelihood of troubled projects occurring and you will make better decisions on which projects to support.

On the one hand, I completely agree. The alternative is chaos. On the other hand, I must ask myself: Why, then, are most of my Guerrilla projects done for Fortune 1000 companies—many of which have deep roots in all the PMO basics?

My answer is simple: No methodology, bureaucracy or board can completely overcome the folly of organizational politics, resistance to change and a basic fear of telling the truth.

If you couple the political dynamics with the root causes of project failure listed on page 17, you can see that the demise of some projects will simply be outside the control of any one person or process. Imagine further if there are multiple projects vying for the attention of the same resources. Before long, you're facing the perfect storm and the wind is about to snap the mast.

In other words, even in the most vigilant and mature organizations, troubled projects are simply going to happen. GPM focuses on how to respond to a troubled project. But here are a few tips for executives on how to *prevent* troubled projects:

- **Keep an eye on your high-priority projects by reviewing the Guerrilla Justification Criteria at least quarterly.** Over the years, I've received feedback from IT executives who have continued to use the criteria as one of the most valuable leave-behinds after a turnaround project. Careful consideration of the criteria on a regular basis will enable you to catch the problems which can sneak by standard gate reviews and status reports.

- **Use Guerrilla Results Initiatives to reduce risk and identify core value quickly.** Before NASA landed a man on the moon, they sent un-manned space modules to orbit the moon. Then they sent manned space modules. Then they landed on the moon. Too often, we organize big projects without ever orbiting the moon first. The concept of a Guerrilla Results Initiative is to deliver a small piece of the overall project end-to-end, thus encountering many of the same obstacles and decision points that a larger project would. By doing this rapidly in a small chunk, the team can easily rally behind a solution. Overall, executives tend to shoulder too much risk with large projects.

- **Reduce your overall risk by doing fewer dependent projects in parallel.** In legacy architectures, there are often hidden dependencies between databases and systems which can derail a project suddenly. You can avoid this risk by simply setting the customer's expectations early. Show them the importance of delivering one project before attempting to implement another.

- **Circle back with routine triage, not just crisis triage.** The requirements, assumptions and benefits of a project can obsolete themselves quickly. Most projects take more than six months to complete. Re-examining the original drivers behind the project can be illuminating and does not take long.

- **Go to the scene — give the project fewer places to hide.** The best way to do this is through a hands-on progress check. Ask to see what has been produced thus far. Do not depend entirely on the status reports coming from your management team. Have coffee occasionally with team members, giving them a one-on-one opportunity to express their opinions about the project.

- **Don't shoot the messenger.** Bad news is a sign of transparency, which is a sign of good health in an organization. To re-enforce this concept, send out emails occasionally in which you thank individuals for catching certain problems. Blaise Pascal, a 17th century mathematician and philosopher, once wrote: "The last thing one knows is what to put first." By seeking early awareness of risks and problems, you move ever closer to knowing what to put first.

- **Use agile development methods where appropriate.** Agile methodologies have not proven themselves to scale well on large projects. On smaller projects, bug fixes or enhancements, however, they can be highly useful. Guerrilla Results Initiatives (page 11) are a good example of this. Further, the core concepts of Agile methodologies are appropriate regardless of scope. Among those concepts are close involvement with the customer/end-user, rapid feedback and course correction ("fail fast, fail cheap"), and chunking the project into manageable iterations. These concepts should be integrated into a project regardless of the methodology required by the organization.

- **Seek redundancy in vital business knowledge and skill sets.** Not only is this a safety measure for the business, but it inspires more creative thinking and helps prevent the stifling occurrence of information hoarding. I have seen entire projects held hostage by one or two knowledge resources.

- **Reduce complexity constantly.** It's not exciting, and the business itself rarely appreciates the significance of it, but complexity reduction has a bigger potential pay-off than nearly any project. If possible, use large internal project requests (such as building a new Accounts Receivable system) as a justification to move toward Master Data Management approaches. A common example of this in a large organization is the consolidation of multiple customer data models into fewer systems, or even one — leading to an improvement in agility and a reduction in maintenance overhead.

Conclusion—Flight of the Phoenix

In the introduction of this book, I alluded to the use of canaries in coal mines as a warning system. As I conclude this book, I am struck by the relevance of another winged creature — the mythological phoenix. As legend holds, once every 500 years, the phoenix immolated himself on a nest of aromatic branches. Then, over a period of three days, a baby phoenix evolved from the ashes of the nest. It is this quality of self-renewal in the phoenix which has represented hope in many forms throughout history — even on the patches of WWII bomber jackets.

One of the most interesting dynamics on a Guerrilla project is the transition period between doubt and hope. When people start to believe, "Hey, we're really going to fix this thing!," they have a whole new strut about them. They start to laugh again. They start to invest themselves more fully. As a Guerrilla PM, that period — and knowing that you had a hand in it — is one of the most gratifying moments on the project.

Today's projects are fraught with increasing complexity, unpredictable changes and a high-margin for error — all the canaries of our project management coalmine. With projects moving at such high velocity, it's easy to overlook the warning signs before it's too late for simple fixes.

The good news, as we hope you've ascertained from this book, is that Guerrilla Project Management can help you rescue troubled projects. It can help you mitigate risk, expedite development, reduce mistakes and get projects back on track.

With Guerrilla Project Management, a project can rise from the ashes and fly toward renewal — just like the phoenix.

About the Author—Shane A. Hills, PMP®, CTP

Shane A. Hills, PMP®, has served as the program manager – leading and mentoring teams of project managers – on more than two dozen high-profile business transformation initiatives. A short list of his clients includes Xerox, Hallmark, Sprint, Bank of America, Associated Wholesale Grocers, H&R Block and the USDA's Risk Management Agency. He has led teams of 10-100 resources, with profit-and-loss responsibility on programs ranging from $1m-$50m.

Shane is the president and founder of Tech21, Inc., a systems integration consultancy located in Overland Park, Kan. (a suburb of Kansas City, Mo.). He is a frequent speaker at industry conferences, and often quoted in the media on the subject of project recovery.

Shane is also a Certified Turnaround Professional (CTP), a designation which requires comprehensive exams on turnaround management, bankruptcy law, and accounting and finance. Fewer than 1,000 professionals hold the CTP, many of them CPA's, attorneys and consultants from top-tier firms. While the CTP designation is oriented toward corporate turnarounds, many of the same principles apply (and are reflected in) *Guerrilla Project Management*.

Shane divides his time between conducting turnaround assessments, serving as an expert witness on lawsuits involving program failure, and the hands-on management of IT programs and transformation initiatives. Observing the need to "pick up where the traditional methodology stops," Shane created *Guerrilla Project Management*.

Shane graduated from the University of Kansas in 1988 with a B.S. in Journalism. For the first five years of his career, he was a journalist, business analyst, technical writer and direct mail copywriter. In 1991, he appeared on radio and television talk shows across the country to promote a book he wrote on how to put yourself through college. The first projects he managed in the early 1990s involved direct mail campaigns for banks to sell pre-approved credit cards, home equity lines of credit and automobile loans.

Since then, he has managed programs involving virtually all facets of an enterprise, including cyber security, human resources, inventory management, accounting and finance, customer relationship management, infrastructure management, telecommunications networks and marketing. His projects have run the gamut—everything from custom-built Java and .NET solutions to the complex integration of ERP and CRM systems.

Shane is a certified ScrumMaster and certified in ITILv3 Foundations. He is an excellent technology translator, working as the liaison between technical professionals and non-technical customers, executives and end-users. He is highly experienced in IT portfolio management, complexity reduction, and the principles of master data management.

His favorite activities outside of work include spending time with his wife and family, amateur natural bodybuilding, writing screenplays, and reading books on business, history and film. Having grown up in Lawrence, Kan., and graduating from KU, Shane is a devoted Jayhawk.

Services Offered by Tech21, Inc.

Shane A. Hills, PMP, CTP, author of *Guerrilla Project Management*, is also the president of Tech21, Inc. Founded in 1999 in Overland Park, Kan., Tech21 is a systems integration and project management consultancy. Triggered by Y2K demand, the firm began as a recruiting and placement service for contractors and permanent hires. Since then, Tech21 has evolved with a turnaround-centric focus, specializing in the recovery of IT projects and enterprise change initiatives. Tech21 varies in size based on project demand. The primary services offered by Tech21 are:

- Detailed turnaround assessments/action plans
- Hands-on management of mission-critical projects
- Training of project managers, business analysts and developers on the principles of Guerrilla Project Management (usually in preparation for a specific turnaround project)
- Turn-key availability of well-trained resources who can expedite the project for you
- Speeches and break-out sessions at professional conferences and association meetings
- Expert witness services for lawsuits or arbitration involving IT project failure

Bibliography

1. Boddie, John. *Crunch Mode: Building Effective Systems on a Tight Schedule*. Prentice-Hall, Yourdon Press Computing Series, 1987. One of the early pundits of rapid development, Boddie wrote in his preface, ". . . quality and short development times are not mutually exclusive."
2. Brooks, Frederick P., Jr. *The Mythical Man-Month: Essays on Software Engineering*. Addison-Wesley, 1975, then re-released in 1995. Clearly a renaissance soul, Brooks, known as the "father of the IBM System/360," writes with deft clarity and allusions to history, poetry and philosophy.
3. Cagle, Ronald B. *Blueprint for Project Recovery —A Project Management Guide: The Complete Process for Getting Derailed Projects Back on Track*. AMACOM, 2003. A thorough treatise on the subject, referencing templates and processes used in the government and military sectors. 304 pages.
4. Cockburn, Alistair. *Writing Effective Use Cases*. Addison-Wesley, 2001. Cockburn was one of the original signers of the Agile Manifesto in 2001. Like the principles of Agile, Cockburn's book is lean and valuable.
5. Covey, Stephen R. *The 7 Habits of Highly Effective People: Powerful Lessons in Personal Change*. Simon & Schuster, 1989. Two of Covey's principles, "start with the end in mind," and "make sure the main thing is the main thing," are reflected in *Guerrilla Project Management*.
6. Feld, Charlie. *Blind Spot: A Leader's Guide to IT-Enabled Business Transformation*. Olive Press, 2009. As CIO at Frito-Lay in the 1980's, Feld led an IT transformation which continues to be used today as a case study for Harvard Business School. Feld's skill as a leader and communicator—and his ability to simplify technology objectives—make this book a must-read for IT recovery managers.
7. *Harvard Business Review on . . .* The HBR books are written in a pragmatic and useful manner, utilizing case studies and providing high-quality ideas. In particular, I have focused on the following topics from HBR: *Leading Through Change, Negotiation and Conflict Resolution, Collaborating Across Silos, Managing Yourself, Managing Projects, Effective Communication*, and *Turnarounds and Acquisitions*.
8. Hoberman, Steve. *Data Modeling Made Simple: A Practical Guide for Business & Information Technology Professionals*. Technics Publications, 2005. The success of any systems development project can be directly mapped to the quality of its underlying data. If you are a non-technical executive or project manager, this book is invaluable. It's short and easy to read.
9. Johnson, Jim. *My Life is Failure: 100 Things You Should Know to Be a Successful Project Leader*. The Standish Group International, Inc. 2006. The Standish Group was the first to document, categorize and quantify the causes of project failure. The results of their bi-annual CHAOS reports are widely quoted in industry publications.
10. Kendrick, Tom. *Identifying and Managing Project Risk: Essential Tools for Failure-Proofing Your Project*. AMACOM, 2009. An excellent resource on the subject of assessing, monitoring and controlling risk.

11. Kliem, Ralph. *Managing Projects in Trouble: Achieving Turnaround and Success*. Auerbach Publications, 2011. Providing numerous flow diagrams and checklists, this book explains how to take action in ways that will increase the likelihood of success and minimize the possibility of failure. 210 pages.
12. Kothari, Dahnu; Mitchell, Romeo. *Managing Business and Project Recovery*. D2i Consulting, 2008.
13. Kotter, John P. *A Sense of Urgency*. Harvard Business Press, 2008. Kotter asserts that one of the biggest causes of failure in enterprise change initiatives (which typically involve a large IT systems development component) is the lack of a sense of urgency. His book provides many examples of this.
14. Kotter, John P.; Cohen, Dan S. *Leading Change*. Harvard Business School Press, 2002. A business classic positioning Kotter as one of the world's leading authorities on business leadership.
15. Kuebler, Al. *Technical Impact: Making Your Information Technology Effective, and Keeping It That Way*. Al Keubler, 2010-2011. Keubler's depth of experience as a CIO for McGraw-Hill, Alcatel, Los Angeles County and AT&T Universal Card Services imbue this book with keen, no-nonsense insights.
16. McConnell, Steve. *Software Estimation: Demystifying the Black Art*. Microsoft Press, 2006. McConnell has also written *Code Complete*, *Rapid Development*, the *Software Project Survival Guide*, and *Professional Software Development*. I own all of these and have found his work to be insightful and well-written.
17. Ong, Bernard. *How to Rescue Failing Software Projects: Practical, Proven Methods that Work*. BookSurge Publishing, 2009. Included is Ong's five-step rescue formula that is used by the author to rescue real-life failing software projects. 144 pages.
18. Purba, Sanjiv; Zucchero, Joseph J. *Project Rescue: Avoiding a Project Management Disaster*. McGraw-Hill, 2004. A good book which provides a step-by-step intervention process, considers the human side of the equation, and recommends useful project audit questions. 384 pages.
19. Robertson, Suzanne; Robertson, James. *Mastering the Requirements Process*. Addison-Wesley, 1999. One of the most commonly referenced causes of project failure is "poor requirements." The Robertsons have written an oustanding book on how to elicit and write effective requirements.
20. Schwaber, Ken. *Agile Project Management with Scrum*. Microsoft Press, 2004. Schwaber was one of the original signers of the Agile Manifesto in 2001. Contains good examples of agile methodologies at work.
21. Simon, Phil. *Why New Systems Fail: An Insider's Guide to Successful IT Projects*. Course Technology, CENGAGE Learning, 2011. Simon's book delves into great detail about the causes of failed systems development projects, and provides a sound framework for implementation from start to finish, including maintenance and vendor agreements. 384 pages.
22. Smith, John M. *Troubled IT Projects: Prevention and Turnaround*. Institution of Electrical Engineers, 2001. As an experienced project manager, project auditor and strategic consultant, Smith provides a highly readable book which addresses the root causes of project failure interspersed with short, relevant stories from his own experience. 240 pages.
23. Willams, Todd C. *Rescue the Problem Project: A Complete Guide to Identifying, Preventing and Recovering from Project Failure*. AMACOM, 2011. Williams has written an excellent book on IT project recovery, including detailed comparisons of Agile, Critical Chain and traditional waterfall (or "classical") methodologies. 277 pages.
24. Young, Ralph R.; Brady, Steven M.; Nagle, Jr., Dennis C.; *How to Save a Failing Project: Chaos to Control*. Management Concepts, 2011. The authors provide guidance to develop a project plan, establish a schedule for execution, identify project tracking mechanisms, and implement turnaround methods to avoid failure and regain control. 234 pages.
25. Yourdon, Edward. *Death March: The Complete Software Developer's Guide to Surviving "Mission Impossible" Projects*. Prentice-Hall, Yourdon Press Computing Series, 1997, 1999. Yourdon recommends that you do NOT read his book if you are looking for "how things should be done in an ideal world where rational men and women make calm, sensible decisions about the budget, schedule, and resources for your software project."

NOTES